dog
SHOW

Molly RUSSELL
VIVIAN Russell

FRANCES LINCOLN

Molly RUSSELL
VIVIAN Russell

FRANCES LINCOLN

The idea for this book arose when my daughter Molly and I happened to catch the Best in Show television coverage of Crufts for the first time. A little Yorkshire Terrier, with silky floor-length hair and a red velvet bow stuck to the top of its head, shimmered across the green carpet under the spotlights. On the other end of the leash was a man dressed in a tuxedo, running alongside the dog with perfect synchronicity. More sleek and swanky dogs swept in, all exuding star quality and supreme showmanship. We glanced over at our muddy Wire-haired Dachshunds indolently sprawled by the fire and sighed. Even so, there was something quite bizarre about the makeover of one's pet Yorkie into an exotic showpiece puppet, that was, at the same time, visually compelling. We decided we had to photograph this and took our cameras to Crufts the following March.

We were dazzled by its scale and scope. Here was a huge congregation of people symbiotically bound to their dogs in a way that was controlling but also wonderfully affectionate. Poodles, Afghan Hounds, Bedlington Terriers and Pekingese patiently submitted to being obsessively bound up, brushed and blow-dried into elaborate confections, and stared into our lenses with soulful, resigned eyes. We were equally mesmerized by the owners. Some became as one with their dogs through carefully orchestrated outfits, make up and hair. In others the resemblance was more natural. We also found that opposites attract.

But it was the humanity of it all which intrigued and beguiled us most. We loved the extraordinary cast of characters, the quirky juxtapositions, the beauty of so many tactile, tender moments and of life caught on the fly. The public arena of Crufts allowed us to take pictures without feeling intrusive. Press cameras were everywhere and working as a team made us braver. The owners were there to show off their dogs and were as proud to be photographed as the dogs were anxious to please them.

We wondered what we would find at the smaller, less competitive shows that welcome cross breeds and involve children, so we visited the East End of London and the north of England. In choosing a single breed show, it had to be corgis. As the pictures came in, rich in social nuance, we realized we had a book of theme and variation, in which everything was the same, yet everything was different. And so we went further afield. We were curious to see what a French dog show would be like, and went to Dieppe, where we found a microcosm of France, distinctly French in its detail, and to a more European show in Paris. The Westminster Show at Madison Square Garden, New York, the most patriotic of all the shows, captured the exuberant, showbiz style that America excels at.

There are of course, undercurrents of angst, jealousy and disappointment running through the championship shows. For professional breeders the stakes are high. Everyone else wants to bask in the reflected glory of their winning dog. No one likes to lose. The dogs don't mind, though, and always do their best. If only people were as loyal and tolerant with each other as their dogs are with them, the world would be a far happier place.

Vivian Russell

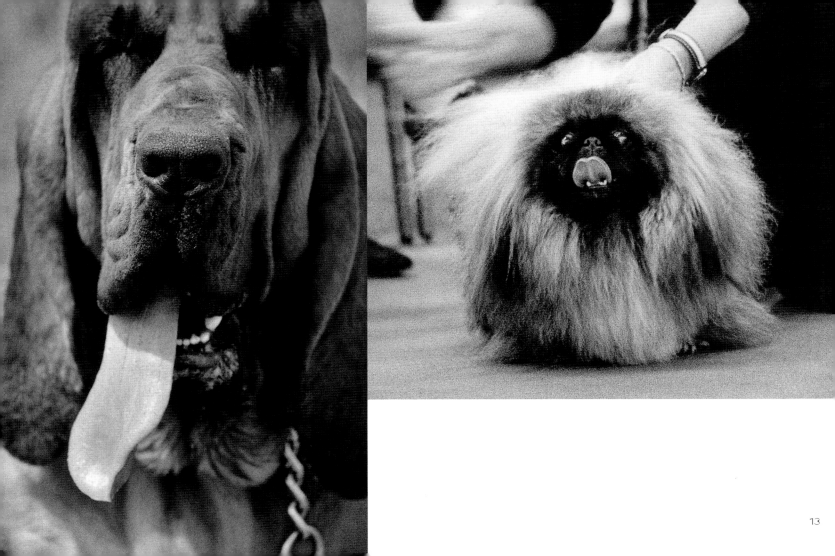

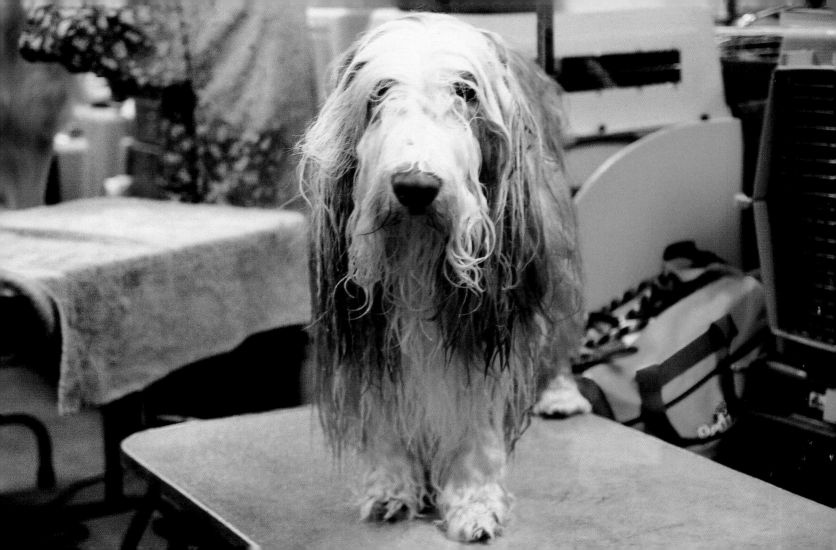

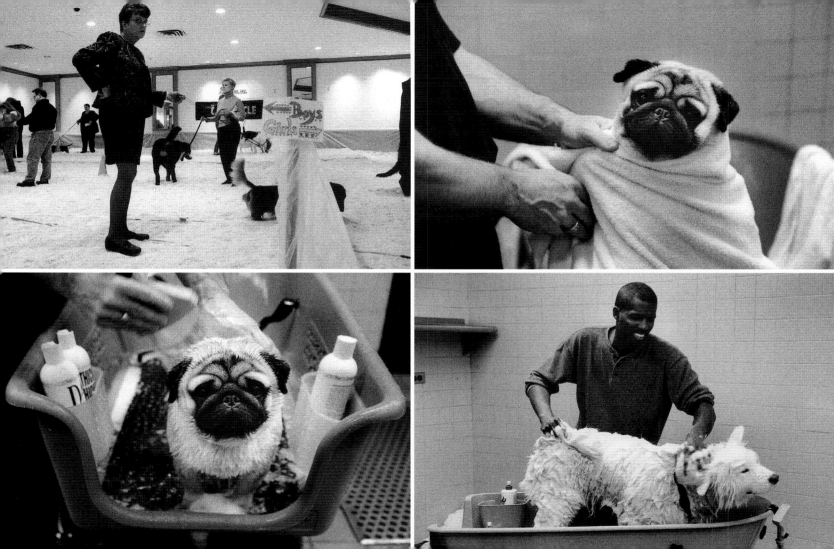

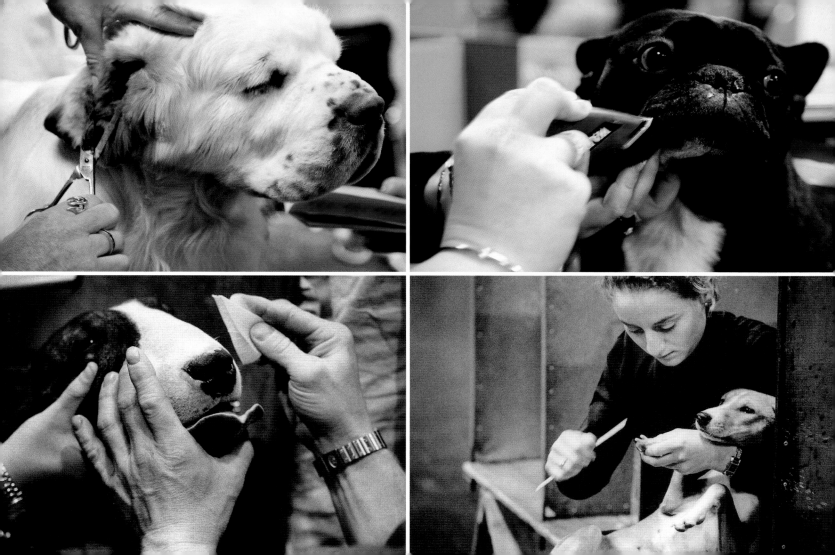

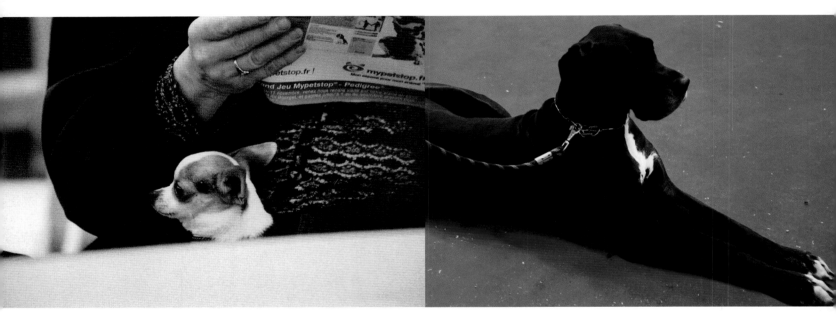

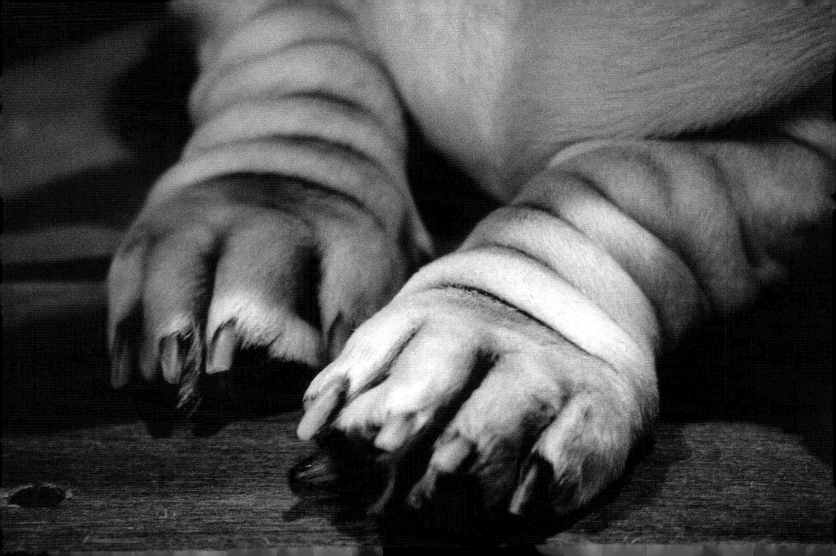

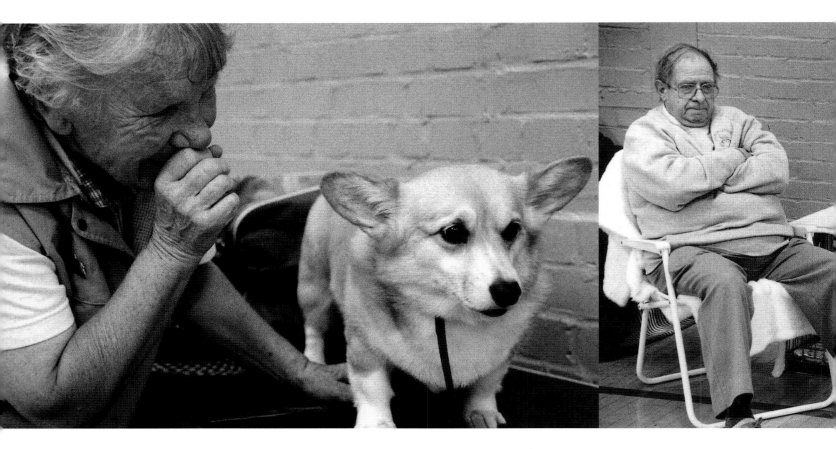

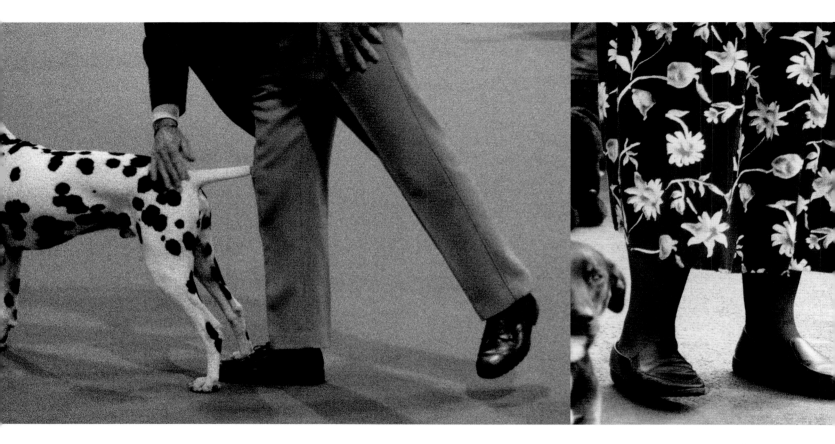

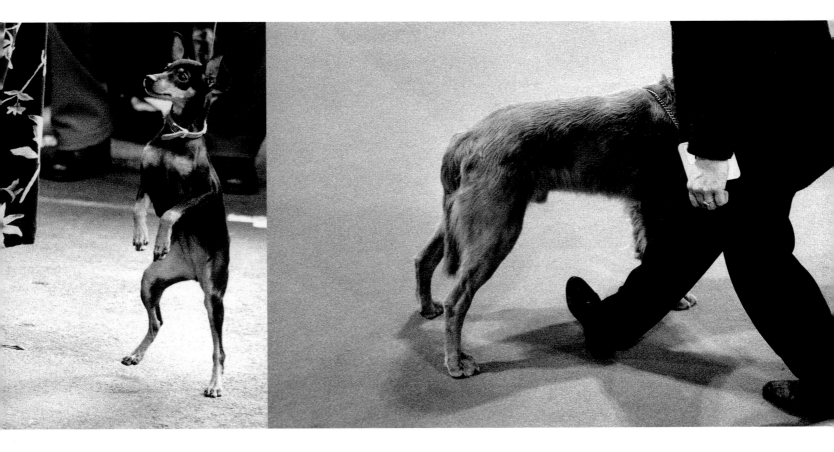

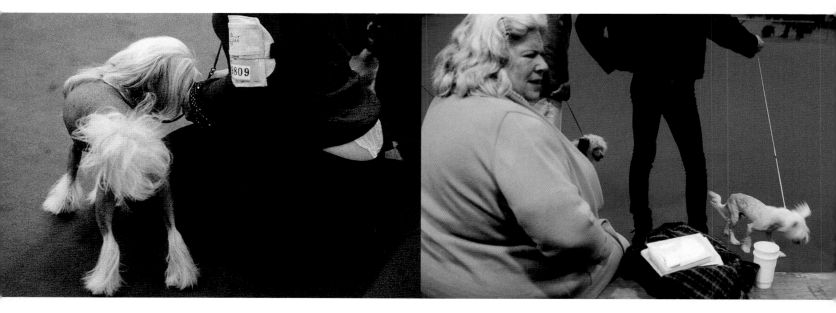

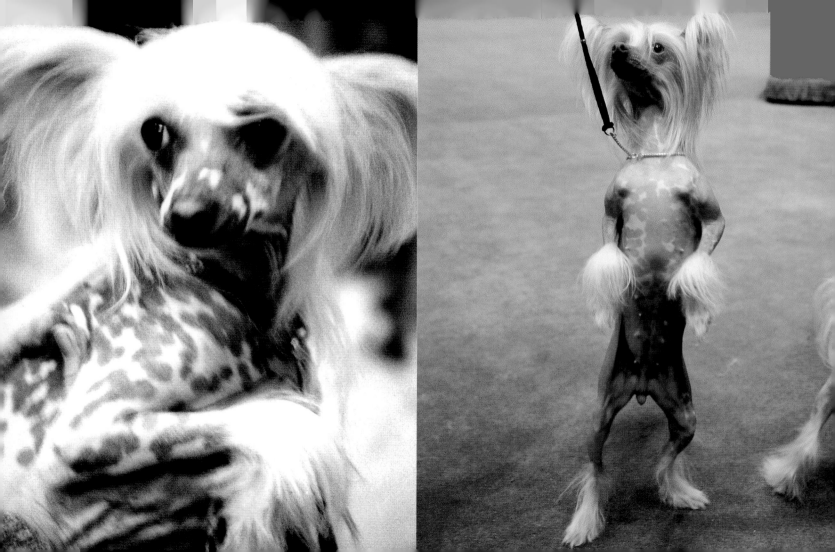

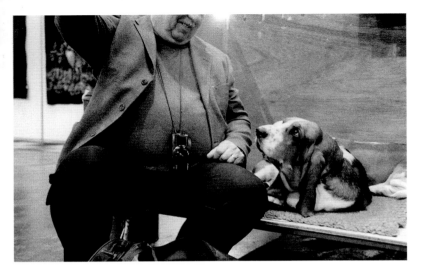

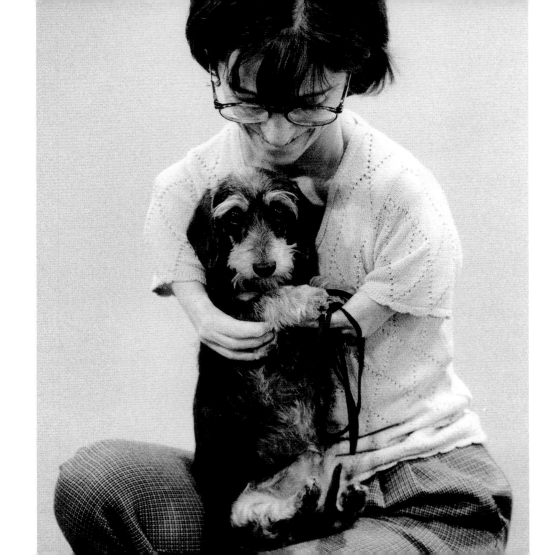

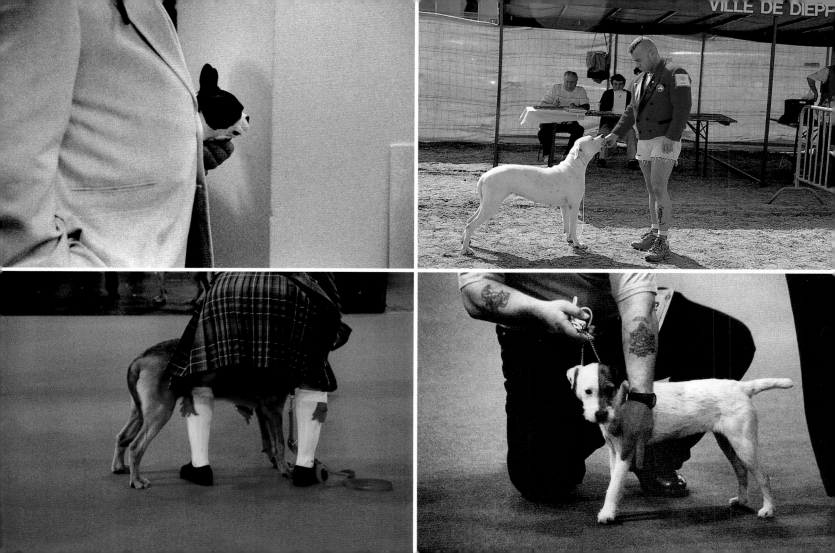

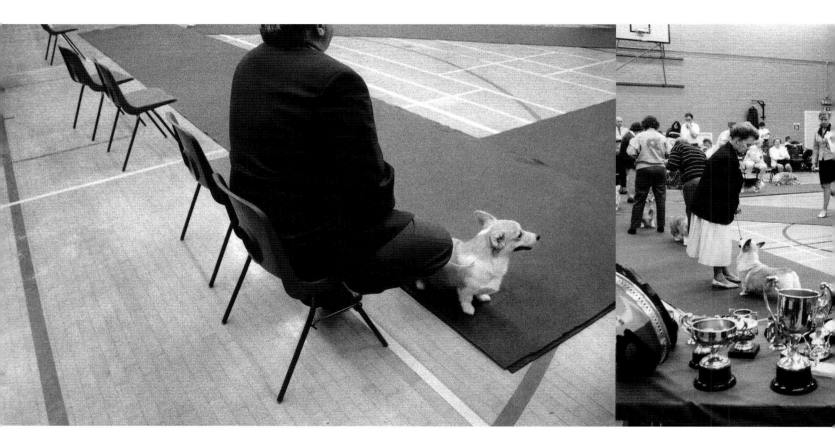

89

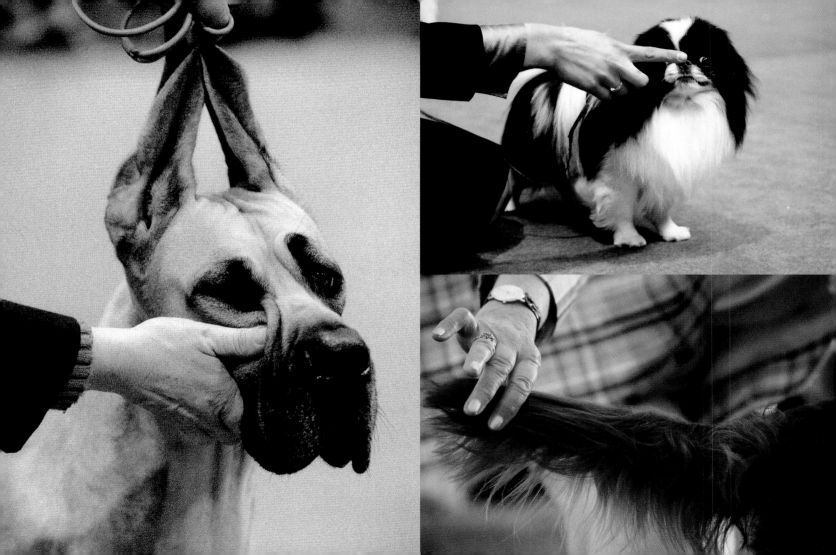

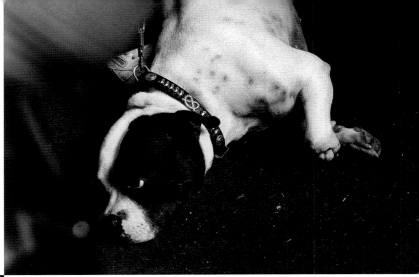

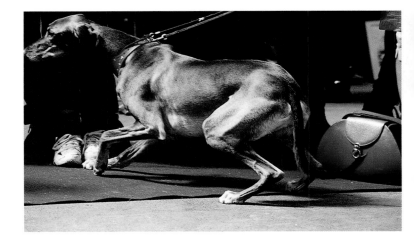

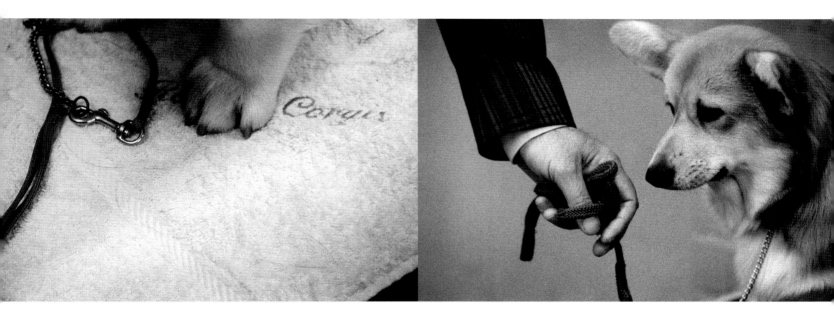

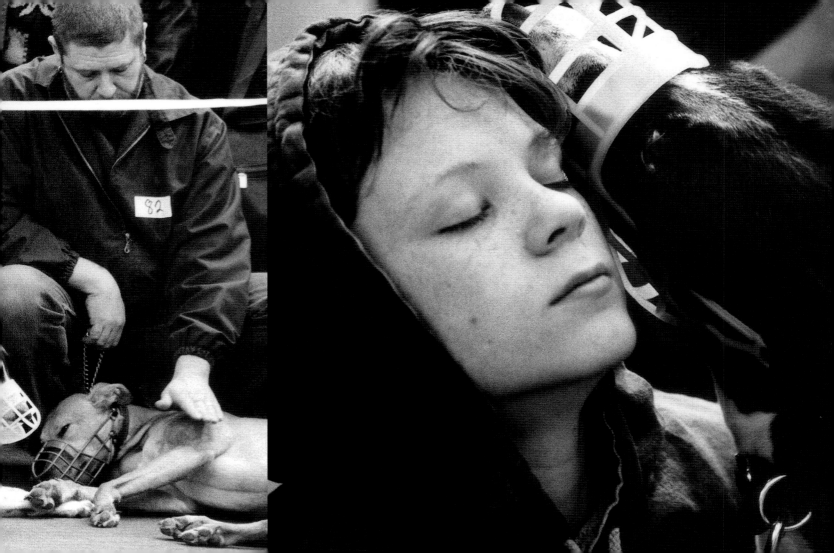

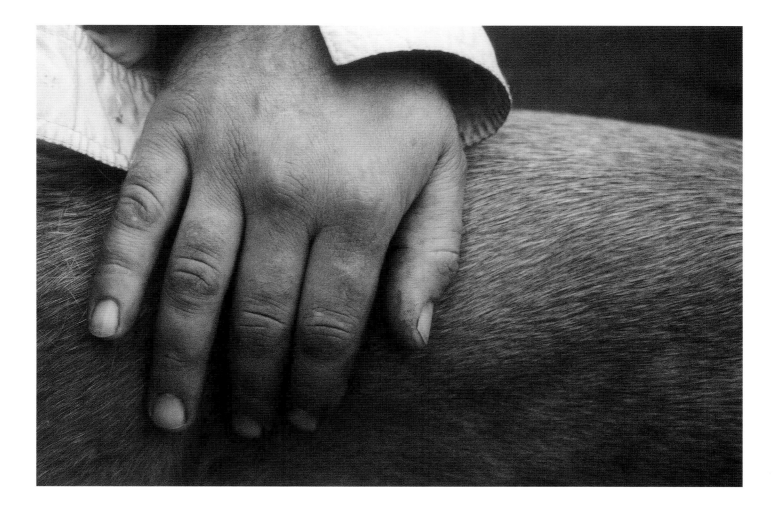

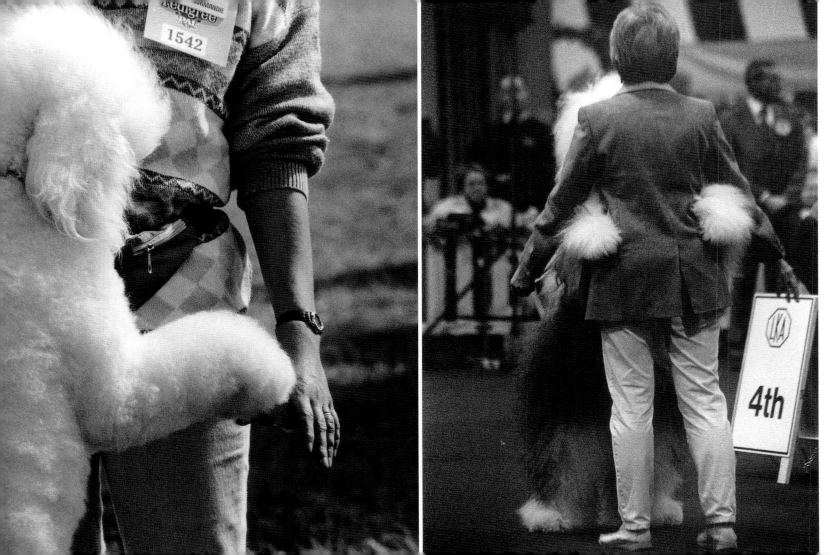

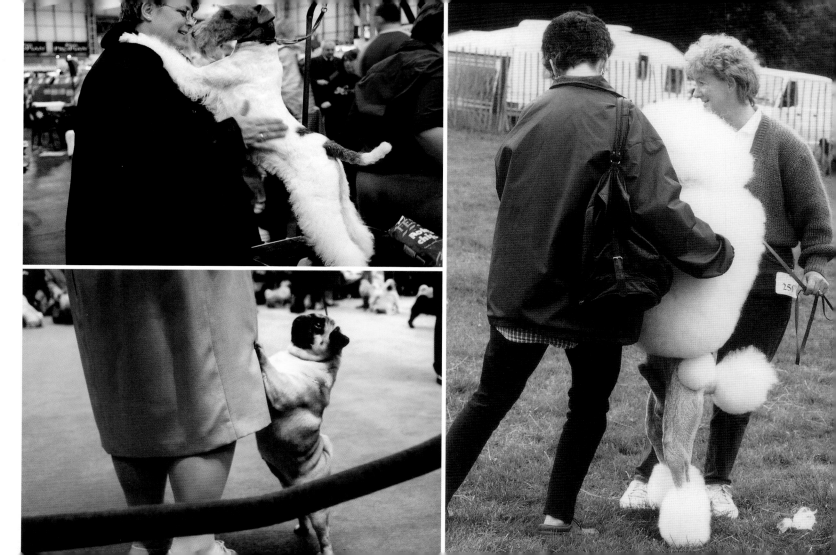

p.68 Left: Chinese Crested Dog, Paris **Right:** Chinese Crested Dog, LKA

p.69 Left: Chinese Crested Dog, Crufts **Right:** Chinese Crested Dog, Westminster

p.70 Above left: Basset Hound, Crufts **Above right:** Pointer, Paris **Below left:** Dachshund, Paris **Below right:** Poodle, Westminster

p.71 Irish Wolfhound, Crufts

p.72 Dachshund, LKA

p.73 Dachshund, LKA

p.74 Above left: Boston Terrier, Westminster **Above right:** Dogo Argentino, Dieppe **Below left:** Bloodhound, LKA **Below right:** Parson Jack Russell Terrier, LKA

p.75 Left, above: Terrier crosses, Morecambe **Left, below:** Bedlington Terrier, Paris **Right:** Border Collie, Scarborough

p.76 Old English Sheepdog, Crufts

p.77 West Highland White Terrier, Westminster

p.78 Left: Poodle, Paris **Right:** Chinese Crested Dog, Paris

p.79 Left: Yorkshire Terrier, Paris **Right:** Yorkshire Terrier, Paris

pp.80-81 Left: Irish Wolfhound, Westminster **Middle:** Great Dane, Scarborough **Right:** Bloodhound, LKA

p.82 Left: Scottish Terrier, Scarborough **Right:** Norfolk Terrier, Westminster

p.83 Left: Chihuahuas, Dieppe **Right:** Labrador Retriever, Morecambe

p.84 Borzoi, Crufts

p.85 Afghan Hound, Crufts

pp.86-7 Welsh Corgis, Corgi Show

p.88 Above: Pekingese, LKA **Below left:** Dachshund, LKA **Below right:** Welsh Corgi, Corgi Show

p.89 Left: Bloodhound, LKA **Right, above:** Bull Terrier, Crufts **Right, below:** Dachshund, Romsey

p.90 Left: Deerhound, Crufts **Middle:** Airedale Terriers, Paris **Right:** Bull Terrier, Paris

p.91 Left: Affenpinscher, Westminster **Middle:** Greyhound cross, Spitalfields **Right:** Whippet, Crufts

p.92 Scottish Terrier, Crufts

p.93 Scottish Terrier, Crufts

p.94 Left: Great Dane, LKA **Right, above:** Japanese Chin, Westminster **Right, below:** Irish Setter, Cumberland

p.95 Above: Curly-coated Retriever, LKA **Below:** Basset Hound, Paris

p.96 Welsh Corgi, Corgi Show

p.97 Greyhound, Spitalfields

p.98 Left: Pomeranian, Cumberland **Right, above:** Pomeranian, Cumberland **Right, below:** Pomeranian, LKA

p.99 Left, above: Pomeranian, LKA **Left, below:** Pomeranian, Cumberland **Right:** Pomeranian, Cumberland

p.100 Left: Ibizan Hound, Crufts **Right:** Borzoi, LKA

p.101 Chinese Crested Dog, Westminster

p.102 Above left: Shar Pei, Paris **Above right:** Staffordshire Bull Terrier, Spitalfields **Below left:** Grand Bleu de Gascoigne, LKA **Below right:** Greyhound cross, Spitalfields

We are indebted to Anne Fraser, without whose staunch support and love of dogs this book may never have been published, and for this reason only is she forgiven for being the devoted owner of Mrs Putzing, who is, I regret to say, a cat! We would also like to thank everyone on the Frances Lincoln team, with special thanks to our brilliant designers, Caroline Clark and Becky Clarke, and to our publisher, John Nicoll. Our thanks also go to the people who have helped us behind the scenes: to Nigel Winfield, who runs the Spitalfields Alternative Dog Show, David Frei at Westminster, Tiffany Daneff, Adam Herbert, subjected to endless hours looking at our pictures, John Hoyland and Nick Downing, Caradoc King and Sam Boyce; to our Pa and Gramps, Harvey Jolly, who has promised to buy lots of copies. We are grateful to our London printers: Stuart Keegan from Just Black and White, Danny Chau, Grade One, Panther Imaging, and Isis, who worked miracles with our high speed film as we don't use flash, and all at Process Supplies for their advice and prompt supply of film. For help with identifying the breeds and cross breeds, our thanks go to our wonderful local Keswick vets, Jean Gilbert and Ron Gilbert, and Hazel Newton at Greta Bank veterinary surgery. We can't resist mentioning the dear old Novotel near Paris and Coventry, which seemed like the only hotel on the planet to welcome our dogs when we started this project six years ago and where we stayed many times photographing Crufts and the LKA, spending our evenings in the lobby chatting up the other dogs. Thanks also to our long-suffering son and brother, Rupert, who was dragged round the shows during his teenage years, consigned to the sidelines and under strict instructions to mind Harry and Lulu. He had his moment of glory, though, on a sunny afternoon in Scarborough, when he rolled up his jeans and won 3rd Prize in 'The Best Six Legs' with Lulu. Third Prize? Well, how could he compete with the chap in a skirt on page 75? Thanks, finally, to our little dachshunds, Harry and Lulu, who inspired this book. Had it not been for the twelve years they've shared our lives, we would never have known how to take the pictures.

Frances Lincoln Ltd
4 Torriano Mews
Torriano Avenue
London NW5 2RZ
www.franceslincoln.com

Dog Show
Copyright © Frances Lincoln Ltd 2004
Text and photographs copyright © Vivian and Molly Russell 2004

A catalogue record for this book is available from the British Library.
ISBN 0 7112 2258 4

Printed and bound in Singapore
9 8 7 6 5 4 3 2 1